JN093310

観測者の杜

藤山邦子

写真　館野二朗

川のせせらぎ、森の樹々の間を吹き抜けていく風

木漏れ日に揺らぐ草花、寄せては返す海辺の波

草原に舞う蝶や鳥たちの群れ、降り注ぐ雨

太古の昔から人は連綿と続く自然の営みから

様々なことを識り、そして学んできました。

始まりのはじまり

なぜ、私たちは生きているのだろう——。

生命の神秘について考えるとき、その源がこの宇宙全体にあまねく存在する原子にあることが分かると、なにもかもが魔法のように思えてきます。

素粒子が原子をつくり、原子が集まって分子をつくり、分子がさまざまに組み合わさって生きとし生けるものの細胞、組織、臓器をつくる。

そしてどのレベルにおいても、単なる部分の総和ではない新しい性質が生み出されているのです。

小さなものがより大きなものを形づくり、別の新たな性質を生み出すという階層構造。

それこそが私たちの世界を形成している基本原理なのかもしれません。

そして、その階層を辿っていくと〈存在〉の始まりは〈ひとつ〉に帰結します。

私たちの生に意味があるとすれば、その〈ひとつ〉にも意味がある。

つまりすべてに意味があるということ。

It all has meaning.

そんな言葉から本書を始めたいと思います。

森からのメッセージ

Something you need

森の中を歩いていると
ふと鼻先をかすめていく風に
あるいは淀んだ空気に
その匂いが溶け込んでいることに
気づくことがある

熟れた果実の甘酸っぱい香り
それはお腹が空いているとき

心が満たされているときは
鮮やかな花の香り

川のせせらぎを探しているはず
あなたの耳は
それは喉が渇いているとき
水の匂いを感じたら

そんなふうに
森はいろんな形で
メッセージを送り
あなたが必要としているものを
教えてくれるのです

お天道様

Made in heaven

小さな舟に乗って
長い川を下っていく――
途中にはよい流れ
悪い流れがあるでしょう

流れが乱れたり滞ったりしたときは
目の前の障害物だけに囚われず
空の上から自分を眺めること

自分を超えた大いなる存在に思いを巡らすこと

自然には善も悪もありません

ただ一つ正しいと言えることは
自分の心の声に従って
「より善く生きよう」とする姿勢でいること
お天道様に恥ずかしくない生き方を心がける
そうすればいつかはきっと乗り越えられる

お天道様は
そんなふうに世界を作っているのです

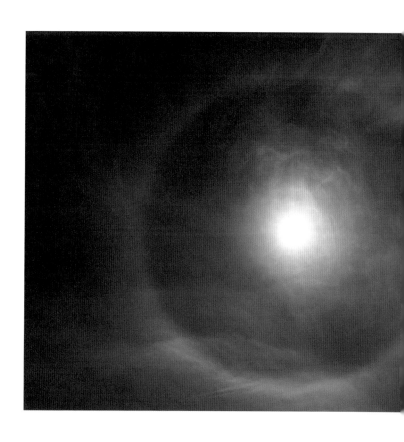

虹のハーモニー

Gift from the universe

雨上がりの空に顕れる虹
雲からの和音が調うかのよう
この宙（そら）からの贈り物を
毎日この地球のどこかで
虹を見上げている誰かがいる
虹は調和の象徴
鳥が囀（さえず）り合って
ハーモニーを奏でるように
私たちも互いを
優しく鼓舞し合えたら
どんなに素敵なことでしょう

海と大地と

Waiting for the sunrise

未明の浜辺
打ち寄せる波の呼吸
息を合わせて裸足で歩く
サクサクと砂が鳴く音と
波の音が重なって
ひとつのリズムをつくりだす
サクサクザブーン
サクサクザブーン
濃紺の空に
煌めく星たち
その下の水平線の向こうには
うっすらと絵筆を引いたような

朝の光のグラデーション

私はその場で足を止めて

静かに身体を横たえ

目を閉じて

その声を聴く

大切なのは全身を耳にすること

身体中の細胞を

ひとつ残らず鼓膜に変えて

大地と海が交わす

美しく饒舌な言葉のリズムに

耳を澄ませる

朝日を待ちながら

さんずい

Shape of water

光と風の加護によって
命の源は護られ
長い歳月を
流転しながら
液体、気体、そして固体と
三態変化を繰り返す
水はすべての命のおおもと
太陽の光が露を生み
雫となって
地上に繁みを栄えさせる

水は大地を洗い清め・・
濯ぎ浄化し、そして潤す・・

私たちが流した涙も汗も・・
すべては水に戻り・
河から海洋へと還っていく・・
水はすべての源・
さんずいの不思議
・・・

名も知らぬ花

As it is in the field

野辺に咲く花

摘みとって

花瓶に差して飾るより

野にあるそのままの姿が

もっとも美しい

森にいると

それを心の底から

実感する瞬間があります

名前をすぐに調べなくてもいい

「美しい」とか　「可愛い」とか　「可憐」

だといった言葉で

修飾することなく

ただそこにあるがままの

花の在りようを愉しむのです

万象是我師<ruby>万象是我師<rt>ばんしょうこれわがし</rt></ruby>

この世界に存在するもの

すべてに意味があり

すべてから学ぶことができる

そう念じているだけで

明日からの世界は

これまでとは別の貌<ruby>貌<rt>かお</rt></ruby>を

見せてくれるでしょう

心のノイズが
消えないときは

A moment of stillness

なにか決断をするとき
自分の心の声を聴くために
じっと目を閉じて
耳を澄ませる

それでもときどき
うまくいかないことがある
それは雑念と呼ばれる
心のノイズのせい
ラジオを聴くためには
周波数を合わせなければ
雑音しか聞こえない

そんなときは
森を歩く

枯れ葉を踏みしだく足音
鳥や虫たちの声
木々の間を吹き抜けていく風の音
遠くから潮騒も聞こえてくる

そうやって森の音にまみれているうちに
ふと心に圧倒的な静けさが
訪れる瞬間がある
それが自然の
ノイズキャンセリングシステム

宇宙の森の観測者

Where beauty is expressed

深い深い宇宙の森
樹々になる星の配置を観測する

星と星の距離の均衡
集まり輝く河や雲
遠く離れてまたたく光の粒
美の発現するところ
流転する遠い記憶

愛し愛されるための
宇宙の表現
互いを生かし
生かされる
大いなる存在への
畏敬と憧れ
神秘に馳せる想い
昇華する
美のフォルム

涙の波

Whispers from the Deep

砂の上にくり返し
低いうなりをあげて
打ち寄せる銀色の波
波の音は
深海からの遠いささやき
魔法使いの呪文のよう
時間の概念を
不確かなものにしてしまう
目の前の光景は

海と陸の境界
陸を浚おうとする
変幻自在の砂の音
風と海が力を合わせ
幾重も時を超え
私たちに語りかけてくる
想像をかきたて
時空を紡ぐ寓話の軌跡に
想いを馳せる

あの銀色の波をつくっているのは
これまでに流されてきた無数の涙

ふたつの森
Forest full of wonders

朝早くに起き出して
森の散歩から
戻ってきたふたりの息子に
「森はどうだった?」
お母さんが尋ねました

「あちこち虫だらけで……」
がっかりしたように肩を落とす長男

次男は表情を輝かせて
いろんな鳥や虫がいたこと
きれいな花が咲いていたこと

苔で足を滑らせて転びそうになったことなど

いつまでも話をやめようとしません

長男の目には 「虫だらけの森」

次男の目には 「驚きに満ちた森」

ふたりの子どものうち

有意義な朝のひとときを過ごせたのは

どちらだったでしょう

ひとつの 〈嫌い〉 や 〈苦手〉 に囚われて

他のものまで目に入らなくなってしまうのは

あまりにももったいないことです

感情の波

Stand up again

不穏な海鳴りと共に
打ち寄せてくる大波
流されまいと
必死で抗うその足を
小石まじりの激流が
容赦なく削っていく
それでもあなたが
痛みに耐えられるのは

たとえどんな波でも
いつか必ず引いていくことを
知っているから
それでも耐えられなくなったら
いっそ波に身を投じればいい

ただひとつだけ守るべきことは
どんな濁流にもみくちゃにされていたとしても
しっかりと目を開き
自分自身から目をそらせないこと
そうすれば
再び波が引いたとき
あなたはすぐに立ち上がれるから

大きく
息を吸って

Nature has the answer

私たちがこの世界に生まれて
最初にすること

それは息をすること

だから「生きる」ということは

「息をする」ということなのです

シンプルに見えて

その仕組みはとても複雑です

呼吸だけではありません

生命が保たれているのは

私たちの身体を造る

数十兆個の細胞で繰り返される

1秒間に何万回何十万回という

化学反応のたまもの
その仕組みのほとんどを
人間は知りませんが
私たちの身体——自然——は
この地球に誕生したときから
答えのすべて知っているのです

悲しみに沈み込んでいるその最中でも
あなたの身体の中では毎日
一兆個もの細胞が死に
同じ数の細胞が生まれています
その奇跡を忘れないで生きましょう
さあ、大きく息を吸って！

ほんとうの強さ
The strength nature demands

誇らしげにそびえ立ち
枝葉を広げていた大木が
嵐や大雪に耐え切れずに
折れ、倒れていく
その一方で少しの風でも
いつもゆらゆらと頼りなさそうに揺れている
柳の木は多少の強風や大雪くらいでは倒れません
自然が求めるのはほんとうの強さ

どんなことにも一本気に
真正面から向かっていく
剛直な強靱さより

苦難や危機に直面しても
それに柔軟に対応して乗り切る
しなやかさのほうが尊い

だから本当に強い人は優しいのです

いつもの一日

Turn off the autopilot

いつもの散歩道
考え事しながら歩くうちに
気がつけばもう家の前
いつもの通勤路
何も考えずただただ歩く
ふと目を上げたら
もう会社の前

どうしてだろう

毎日が新しくて

好奇心にあふれていた子供時代

それが大人になっていくにつれ

毎日太陽が届けてくれる新しい一日は

「いつもと同じ毎日」になり下がり

ルーティンワークの積み重ね

見る、聞く、話す、笑う、相槌を打つ

歩く、食べる、息をする

仕事も家の戸締まりも

生活はすべて無意識という名の

〈自動操縦装置〉にお任せ

人は自分の足あとを
気づかないうちになぞる生き物
その無数の足あとがいつの間にか
深い轍となり
その溝に沿って動くようになる
ここらでいったん立ち止まって
自動操縦モードを解除してみましょう
さて、あなたのスイッチはどこ？

愛のかたち

Love over time

たとえば犬と猫、ヒツジと馬、豚とアヒル……

種族を超えた動物同士のじゃれ合う姿や

いたわり合い助け合う姿には

とても心がなごみます

ライオンとシマウマのように

食べる側と食べられる側だった場合などは

深い感動すら覚えます

人と人が生命を奪い合う戦場で

敵どうしの兵士が手を取り合う姿

長年敵対し合っていた

国と国の人々が抱擁を交わす姿

ベルリンの壁が崩れ落ちた

その瞬間を目にした

世界中の人たちが涙したのも

すべてそこに深い〈愛〉を感じたからでしょう

男女の場合はどうでしょう

男と女も〈性〉を超越した

愛で結ばれることは可能です

そのためには

男女が互いを見つめ合うのではなく

同じ志をもって同じ星を標にすること

見つめ合うのは決意をするとき

恋愛は時間と共に色褪せ

愛は時間と共に深まっていくものなのです

記憶の香り

Memories in the wind

ふとした瞬間
なんだかとても懐かしい匂いが
鼻孔をくすぐっていくことがある
思わずその場で立ち止まり
鼻をくんくんさせてみる

それは遠い昔
子どもの頃に遊んだ

日だまりの草いきれ

公園の砂場
古い木のほこら

なんの匂いだったか
思い出そうとしても
すぐには思い出せない時もある
でもまたいつかきっと
風が運んでくれる
遠い記憶と共に

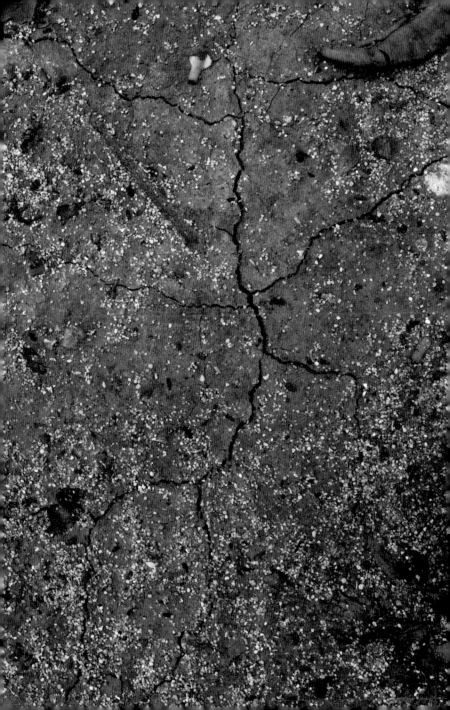

植物のように

For a more fruitful life

地上に生きる個が
宇宙に包まれるとき
存在の孤独が癒やされ
全体の中で息づく

地球に生きるものの中で
最もよく天（そら）の動きを

体現する生命は植物
この地上で生活を営む者として
植物のように天に
心を向けるようになれれば
人生はより実り多いものになる
なのに自然から遠ざかろうとする人々
自然がモニター越しに見るだけの
単なる概念となるのはあまりに悲しい

森の中のクリスマスツリー

Harmony of life form

満天の星の下
森の中から夜空を見上げると
樹々の枝葉のすき間からのぞく
星々の瞬きが
まるでクリスマスツリーのよう
それを見るたびに私は確信します
この宇宙に孤立無援の存在など

なにひとつとして無い

ということを……

宇宙に存在する物質はすべて

〈ひとつ〉から始まっています

私たちの肉体も

この地球から何億光年離れた星も

すべては同じ場所

同じ時間に生まれた

素粒子から創られています

私たちの肉体を構成する何十兆もの細胞が

互いにネットワークで結ばれ

調和しながらひとつの生命体として
在り続けることができるのも
すべての細胞が同じ遺伝子で
つながっているから

宇宙にある無数の星々も
私たちもまた
この世界が誕生した瞬間から
素粒子という
ひとつの鎖でつながっているのです

幸運のおすそ分け

Seeds of fortune

森へ行ったら
木の実が沢山なっていて
カゴいっぱいに採れました
ひとりで食べるには多すぎます
あなたならどうしますか
知り合いや近所の人におすそ分け？
それとも飽きるまでひとりで食べますか？
おそらくほとんどの人が
〈おすそ分け〉を選ぶはず

ひとりでこっそり食べるより
みんなに喜んでもらえたほうが気分もいい
でもこれが〈幸運の種〉だったらどうでしょう
木の実のように分け与えることができますか
あなたが本当に幸運を手に入れられるかどうかは
そこにかかっています

幸運の女神が微笑みかける人とは
ある文豪の言葉を借りるなら
〈分福〉のできる人です
自分に訪れた運気を
惜しみなく人にも与えられる人
独り占めはかえって運気を逃します

あなたが分けた福の種がいつか
芽を出しあなたのもとに再び
返ってくるかもしれません
でもそれは期待しないこと
心を高らかに朗らかに
それがすべての鍵なのです

生命の歓び

Joy of life

いつも私たちの中に在って

森羅万象すべてに宿る

最も深い存在

高次の意志

それらに触れるために

生命の歓びを感じ取ろう

自然を愛でよう

トンボの羽音
宙に漂う蝶々の鱗粉
朝顔の葉の産毛
星のささやき

耳を澄まし目を凝らし
味わい尽くす
身体中の感覚を
生き生きと研ぎ澄ませていく

そんなふうにして得た感覚に誠実でいよう
「生きるため」と他人や自分を偽って
生きるのではなく

雲

原初の波を響かせる水　空の徴と化す

波打ちながら轟き　人々はそれを読み標とした

生命を育む　地球の誕生と共にありし雲

波は根源のダンス

逆まく波のしぶき　雲は気の塊の航跡

空に立ち昇って　宇宙の象徴

雲となり

カブトムシの恩返し

Just want to help, so I do.

昨夜の雨でできた
切り株の水たまりで
溺れかけている
カブトムシを見つけた
そっと指でつまんで
そばの木の枝に掴まらせてあげた
カブトムシはしばらく
毛づくろいをするように
忙しく脚を動かしてから

当たり前のことだけれど

礼も言わず

さよならも言わずに

どこかに飛び去っていった

ただそれだけのこと

目の前で困っている人がいたら

いつもそんなふうに

助けられたらいい

ただ助けたいから助けてあげる

それでじゅうぶん

気づかせてくれた

カブトムシに感謝

生命の祈り

Watch over our children

雷と水と火の精霊よ
われらが祖先よ
われらの心を
寛容と調和に目覚めさせたまえ

太陽と月と星よ
海と森と空気と大地の精霊たちよ
われらが子孫を見護りたまえ

生命の祈りを捧げるとき
大いなる宇宙と自然のもとに
ひざまずきひれ伏せる時
命の光に向かいて
開かれる
祝福と尊い循環に
感謝奉る

風と自転車

Leaves away from branches

川沿いの道を自転車で走る
風は向かい風
火照った頬を
春の香りが撫でてゆく
急げや急げ
強まる風に
身体を前に倒し
ペダルを踏む脚に力を込める

帰り道
スピードを出して
すいすいと走る

なのに風はまるで
動くのをやめてしまったよう
そこで覚るのだ
人は逆風にはすぐ気づくけど
追い風に背中を押されているときは
気づきにくいことを
そして目の前をフワリと横切っていく
落ち葉を見てこう思う
枝から離れた葉っぱには
向かい風も
追い風もないのだって

いまの月いにしえの月

Read the Moon

現代人の多くは
月が地球に与える影響を知っています
でもその知識は
すべて科学によってもたらされたもの

かつて古代の人たちは
月を暦を読むための
目安としてだけでなく
畏敬すべき信仰の対象として見てきました
天文学や物理の知識がなくても

月が自分たち人間や
自然界に与える神秘的な力を
全身全霊で感じ取っていたからです

ひるがえって現代を生きる私たちの中で
それだけの感受性を備えている人が
果たして何人いるでしょう
頭の中の知識はいったん捨てて
古代の人々に想いを馳せながら
ありのままの月を
天体を
自然を
感じ取りましょう

人間の磁場

Magnetic fields of human

コンパスは
深い森の中を歩くときの必需品
子どものとき学校で習った
地球は大きな磁石という話ですが
私たちの地球は棒磁石のような
永久磁石ではなく電磁石
地球の中心部のコアを
溶けた鉄などの金属が
対流する際に生じる電流で
磁場が形成されて
いるのです

私たち人間もそれと同じように
ぶつかり合ったり溶け合ったり
対流しながら
人間の磁場をつくっています
磁場があったおかげで
地球とそこに生きるものたちは
太陽風や強い紫外線から
守られてきたと言われています

私たちが作る磁場も
そうあってほしいと願います

天に地に人に

Pray to the Stars

他者を自分の意のままに

操ろうとする人は

いちばん自由から遠い人

自由な人は

他者をコントロールしよう

とはしないから

自分が不自由だから

他の誰かを動かして
ことを為そうとする
それは無意味なことです

自由とは自らを由として
行動すること
社会におもねず迷惑をかけず
粛々と自分の往くべき道を
歩いていく
それが人としての美しい在り方
最後は手を合わせて
太陽に照らされ
昇華なさいませ

疲れたその身心を
月夜の下で癒しなさいませ
本心からの祈りを星に捧げなさい
千年万年続く祈りが
天に地に人に
届きますように

完璧な存在

Integrity from Within

人はみな裸で生まれる
なにも持たずに生まれる

他の動物もみんな同じ

違うのは人間だけが〈所有〉するということ
食べ物、衣服、住み家、移動手段、装飾品……
ひとりではとうてい持ち切れないほどの
物や財産を手に入れようとする
そして名声や地位といった
実体のないものまでも

動物がなにも持たないまま
生を全うできるのは
生まれたときから

すべてを持っているから

つまり完璧な存在だから

人間だって本当はそう
自分はなにも持ってないと思っていても
本当はその身体の中に小さな宇宙という
〈完璧〉をもっている
なのにいつも何かが足りないと思っている
だからあれもこれも欲しくなる
だからといって持っていることを
恥じる必要はない
なぜならその人は
与・え・る・ことができるから

明日の自分

Me tomorrow

現在から過去を見るように
未来からいまを振り返って見る

明日のいまごろ
今日の自分を
私はどう見ているんだろう

子どもだった頃の私は
いまの私を見て
なにを思いなにを感じるのだろう

いまの自分を形づくった
習慣や物の見方をもう一度見直して
自分の型や殻を破ってみる

（どうせ自分なんか……）

地球上の生き物で
そんなふうに考えているのは人間だけ
どんな生き物も
与えられた生を
ただひたすら全うしている

その姿がとても美しくとても尊い

調和する色

Wavelength of rainbow

秋になると森は
たくさんの色で溢れます
ひと言で〈紅葉〉といっても
葉っぱの色は一枚一枚違います

人の性格や個性もそう
「十人十色」というように

色になぞらえて表現します

異色の顔ぶれ

毛色が違うとか

色が違って見えるのは

それぞれ波長が異なっているから

あの人とは波長が合うとか

合わないとか

よくそんな言い方をします

「波長の合う人どうしだけで

いられれば楽なのに」

などと思いがちですが

世の中はそれでは回りません

この人は波長が違うなと思っても

進んで受け入れましょう

きっとそこに調和が生まれます

虹は色んな波長の光でできているからこそ

美しいのですから

幸せの虫眼鏡

Treasures on the Roadside

散歩に出かけるときは
いつも虫眼鏡をもって出かける
途中見つけた花や草
道端に落ちている
石ころや貝殻
トンボの羽根
気になったものは
手当たり次第
虫眼鏡を近づけて
じっくりと見る・視る・観る

凸レンズの向こうに広がる
知っているようで知らなかった
驚きと感動の世界
見つけたときは
それだけで得をしたような
幸せな気分になる
本物の虫眼鏡がなくても大丈夫
どんな場所にも
必ず幸せの種は落ちています
誰もが心の中にもっている
幸せの虫眼鏡で探しましょう

幻の幸せ
Healing of the Earth

地震、台風、洪水、大雪……
人はそれを災害と呼ぶけれど
大地は自らを修復し
そして自らを癒やす力があります

壊れる多くは人が造ったもの
人工物はさらなる破壊を招きます
次々とコンクリートの層で
覆われていく山や川、そして海岸
生き物たちはしめ出され
居場所を失い
抵抗するすべもなく
静かに滅びていくのです

万物を生成する陰と陽

その陰陽を司る

目に見えぬ壮大な天の動き

畏敬の念を忘れて

己が欲望を満たしたとしても

そこで得られるのは

感動のない幻の幸せ

決して長くは続きません

人は誰でも幸せになることを願います

それは誰にとっての幸せなのか

私たち自身に問いかけるべきときが来ています

生命のダンス

Seize the day

砂浜で星を眺めながら
緑滴る森の懐に抱かれながら
海の深さ空の高さを想像しながら
いつも感じること
それは科学と神話が
決して矛盾するものでも
相反するものでもなく
互いに補完し合うものだということ

私たち人間に与えられた

絶対の自由は

想像する自由

誰にも奪えないその力を

使い尽くしてこそ

人は〈本当〉を見つけられるのです

ある科学者は言いました

――人生には二通りの生き方しかない

ひとつは、奇跡など何も起こらないと思って生きること

もうひとつは、すべてが奇跡だと思って生きること――

宇宙の歴史から見れば

一人ひとりの生など一瞬だとしても

それが連綿と繋がりやがてそれが

悠久の時が大河へと

拡がり続けていくのです

一滴の水が海をつくったように

私たち一人ひとりがまさにいまその奇跡の中に在って

命のダンスをスイングしている状態

それが〈いまを生きる〉ということなのかもしれません

美しい暗闇

Joy of being here and now

感動とは
あらゆる形容詞が蒸発して
頭が動かなくなること
そして心が動くこと

星がまたたく夜だけが
美しいわけではありません

なにもかもが黒く
塗りつぶされた

真っ暗闇も美しい

空に浮かぶ雲も
風に靡く植物も
その姿は見えず
感じるのはただその気配のみ

砂浜を洗う波の音
いまここに在ることの
歓びを教えてくれる

ハテナの芽

Finding hidden beauty

喜びの分かち合いは
知覚の結びつき
万人の心を打つのが
ほんとうの宝
自分だけのものと思った瞬間
それは輝きを失う

自然の中に
秘められた美を

見つけ出そう
与えられることを
待ち望むだけの日々を
終わりにしましょう

感動できる心は
学んで得るものではありません
心にふと浮かんだ小さな〈？〉の芽を
大切に育てていくことから始めましょう

希望の道のり

Shadows on the water's bottom

走り去るように
過ぎていった日々も
駆けてくる未来も
ひとつの空間で
静かに重なり合っている
現在（いま）という新しい次元の入口で
ゆらゆらと揺れる波間に身をゆだね
水底に映る自分の影を俯瞰する

揺るぎない実直さと
しなやかな思考
そしてほんの少しの我侭（わがまま）を混ぜて
希望の道のりを
選択し続けていきたい

また明日

If only I could remember

私にとって過去とは
時間軸から離れて
空間的にもつれ合いながら拡がる
五感の情景

忘却の彼方に去ってしまったことを
いまさらたぐり寄せる必要はないでしょう
それでもこれまで数々の痛みや苦しみを
乗り越えてきた経験が
自分自身だけでなく
家族や友人たちにとって
ほんのわずかでも心の糧となるのならば

こんなに幸せなことはありません
肉体はいつか朽ち果てますが
もし記憶を遺しておくことができたなら

痛みと背中合わせに精一杯生きる人々の姿
無邪気に笑う子供たちの声
水面を渡る潮風の香りと海の蒼さ
どこまでも青い空の清々しさ
生命を謳歌する植物や花のみずみずしさを
心に刻んでおくでしょう

明日もまたお会いしましょう

自分の足で

Go your own way

誰もが歩くその道は
誰にとっても初めての道
途中にはいくつかの分かれ道
どちらの道を選ぶにしても
最初の一歩は
探り足
それでも迷いが
消えないときは
川の浅瀬を歩くときのように
思い切って靴を脱いで
素足になってしまえばいい

あとは風に触れ
流れを掴み
空を仰ぎ星の位置を確かめるだけ

最後まで自分の道を
自分の足で歩く
そう決めたなら
他人を羨むことからも
妬むことからも
解き放たれて
自由に歩けるはず

内なる宇宙

Invisible light

月の光も届かない真っ暗な森

忙しく動き回る動物がいる中

私たち人間は明かりなしでは身動きがとれ
ません

それは私たちが〈見える光〉つまり

可視光線しか知覚できないから

それと同じようにこの宇宙には

人の目には見えない未解明の

事象がそれこそ星の数ほどあるのです

奇跡としか表現のしようがない

人智を超えた絶妙な均衡が働いて

この地球があり生命がある

そのことをいま一度胸に刻んで

日々のことに当たることです

仕事でも私生活でも

なにか事がうまく運ばないというときは

いったん言葉や理屈から離れて

静かに内なる宇宙を眺める

そんな内省の時間をもつことが

必要なのかもしれません

自分を疑う

It's Magic!

舞台の上のマジシャンが
観客のひとりを選んで
これから披露するマジックの仕掛けを
あらためさせる──
よく見かける光景です
こんなときマジシャンが選ぶのは
一見、疑り深くて頑固そうな
「自分の目で確かめたもの以外は信じない」
といったタイプの人

一見、立派な見識の持ち主のようですが

ひとつ欠けていることがあります

それは、もしかしたら自分は見たいものだけを

見ているのかもしれない

と自分自身を疑う視点です

そう信じているからこそそう見える

見えるから信じるのではなく・・・

自分は騙されないと

思いこんでいる人ほど

騙されやすいと言われるのは

そんな背景があるからなのでしょう

「なるほど」と思ったときこそ

両目をこすって目を凝らしましょう

予兆

Always be by your side

私たちがこの世に生まれて
自分の足で立ち上がり
歩き始めるまでに
何度もつまずいたり
転んだりするのは
いつもあなたに手を差し延べ
助け起こしてくれる
人が側にいるのだということを
学ぶためなのかもしれません

大きな挫折をして
もう立ち上がれないかもしれない

そんなふうに思ったときも
あなたを助けてくれる誰かがいる
支えてくれる星や機運がきっと巡ってくる

それは時に
ほんの小さなきっかけや予兆から
始まることがあります
それに気づくか気づかないか
そのわずかな差が
私たちの一生を左右するのです

共鳴

Firm magnetic field

生まれたばかりの赤ん坊にとって
世界は母親の腕の中がすべて

そこから日を追うごとに
少しずつ少しずつ
世界は外へ向かって
広がっていきます
世界が広がるということは

意識が広がる

想像が広がるということ

だからこそ

他人（ひと）の気持ちを察して

共鳴することができるのです

共鳴は磁場を生み出し

それをさらに強くします

その磁場から

万物万象は生じます

共鳴にはプラスの共鳴と

マイナスの共鳴があります

悪事を働く者どうしも
互いに共鳴するという事実を
忘れてはなりません
他人の私欲から出た言動に
かき乱されることのない
強い磁場をつくりましょう

繋がる

God is looking over you

人類に貢献

地球への奉仕

「そんな大げさな」
そう思うかもしれません

でも……
ものごとの大元や本質を問い続けること

探究し続けることはとても大事

常に自分が高い意志とつながっていること
お天道様に見守られていること
それをいつもアタマの片隅に置いておくこと

自分自身があらゆる生命の源泉と繋がり
連鎖していることを
心に想い描くことができれば
たとえどんなに離れていても自らが
祝福し祝福される存在になれるのです

自由の魂
Feelings of freedom

それがもつ
壮大な波動に触れるとき
人は言葉を失い
純粋な精神のみの存在となる

活発な細胞の
生と死のサイクル
精神と肉体の振動が重なり

至高なるレベルの気づきにまで
共鳴現象は起きる

常識で裁くこともなく
意識を限定することもなく
魂の奥底から
本当の自由を感じたとき
畏敬の念が溢れてくるでしょう

いまのあなたは何モード？

Switching operation buttons

電化製品に〈省エネモード〉だとか

〈静音モード〉といった

いろんな運転モードがあるように

私たち人間にもたくさんの○○モードがあります

ひがみモード、恨みモード、怒りモード

過去に失敗をおかしたときのこと

思った通りの結果が出なかったときのことを

思い出してみてください

そのときのあなたは何モードだったでしょう

イライラモード、ひがみモード、それとも弱気モード

それがわかったら今度は

モード切り替えボタンを押すのです

イライラモードで失敗したのなら冷静モードで

恨みモードは大らかモードで

わからないならここはいったん

ニュートラルにリセットして

それからあらためて運転スイッチを

入れればいいのです

切り替えましょう

情報戦

Open your mind

思いやりとは
相手の気持ちを汲むこと
とてもシンプル

駆け引きは
自分を隠して
相手の心の裏を読み
そして利用すること
つまりは情報戦
とても複雑で面倒

だから疲れるのです

仕事も恋愛も人づきあいも

本当の意味で

人と人との距離を近づけるのは

SNSで交わされる

虚飾に満ちた情報などではありません

ヒトはヒト　自分は自分

Facebook、Twitter、Instagram……

スマートフォンのブラウザを閉じて

心を開きましょう

いまあなたのそばにいる人に

不安の正体

Don't be afraid to get hurt

子ども時代の思い出
予防注射の列に並び
自分の順番が来るのを待つ
（痛いのかなあ）
（痛かったらどうしよう）
不安で胸がドキドキする
でも注射が終わってしまえば
ちょっとくらい痛くても
心はずっと軽くなる
あんなに心配して損した
そんな気分になる

傷つくことを恐れているほうが

実際に傷つくよりずっと辛い

なぜなら〈恐れ〉は〈痛み〉よりも

ずっと長く続くうえに

心をむしばむから

怖がっている暇があったら

「エイヤ」と一歩前に

踏み出しましょう

傷ついたら傷ついたとき

だいじょうぶ

きっと薬は見つかります

覚えておいてください

〈傷つく不安〉につける薬はないのです

175

本当の自分

What nature does without knowing it

知らず知らずに重ねた穢（けが）れを
自然は黙って祓（はら）い清めてくれる
自分の自然——本当の自分

取り戻すためには
自分自身の中にある
嘘やごまかし、
奢り、憎しみ、不信に気づくこと
それらは決して
捨て去ることはできない

なぜならそれもまた自然だから
ただ〈在る〉ことから
目を逸らさないこと
自分の過ちを反省できたとき
はじめて本当の自然
本当の自分を取り戻せる

あなたらしく
あるために

Enjoy your true self

ピカピカの食器
ピカピカの靴
ピカピカの窓
ピカピカの笑顔
どんなものでも
ピカピカは気持ちがいい
毎日の暮らしだってそう

輝いていたほうがいいに
決まっています
こびりついた汚れには研磨剤
本当の自分が出てくるまで磨きましょう

よりあなたらしくあるためには
いまの自分を乗り越えなくては

でも磨きすぎにはご用心
疲れてしまって
自分をすり減らしてしまいます
自分磨きもほどほどに

人生の正解

Steady or free?

大海原をゆく二隻の船
一隻は大型客船
安定した船での生活は快適そのもの
もう一隻は小型船
船内の装備は必要最低限
木の葉のように揺れながら
食糧も魚釣りで調達する毎日
しかし航海に緊急事態（トラブル）はつきもの
たとえば突然目の前に
現れた巨大な氷山

すぐに回避できるのは小さな船
大きな船は急な進路変更ができません
あるいは突然発生した大嵐
最寄りの港に緊急避難
そんなとき
小さな船ならどんな港にも入れますが
でも大きな船はそうはいきません

大きな船の安定を取るか
小さな船の気楽さを取るか
それは見栄や世間体ではなく
あなたの〈心〉が決めること
人生に正解はないのです

185

全体を生きる

Accept differences

強い人、弱い人、明るい人、暗い人

頑固な人、融通のきく人

活発な人、おとなしい人

優しい人、意地悪な人……

世の中いろんな人がいて当たり前

だから社会は成り立つのです

たとえば堅牢そのものに見える

建築物も

ゴムから鋼鉄まで

さまざまな性質の材料が使われて

初めてその堅牢さが保てます

相反するものが存在して

はじめて全体が成り立つ

自分とは相反する存在を

異質だとか異物として

排除、拒否してしまうのではなく

受け入れることで

〈全体〉を生きることが

可能になるのです

標なき道を

Back to the Beginning

砂漠を歩くひとりの男
その足取りはのろくて重い
出発するときには
確かに見えていた目印が
いまはもう見えない
自分がどこに向かっているのか
目標に近づいているのか
それとも遠ざかっているのか
それすらもわからない

彼がいますべきことは
砂漠が見渡せそうな
丘の上に登って
再び目標を見つけ出すこと
もしそれでも見つからなければ
勇気を出して
自分の足あとを辿り
目標が見える
場所まで戻ること
そして再び新たな一歩を踏み出すこと

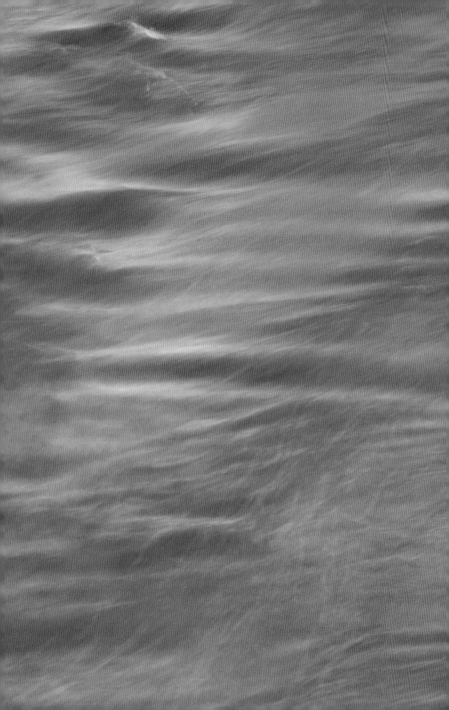

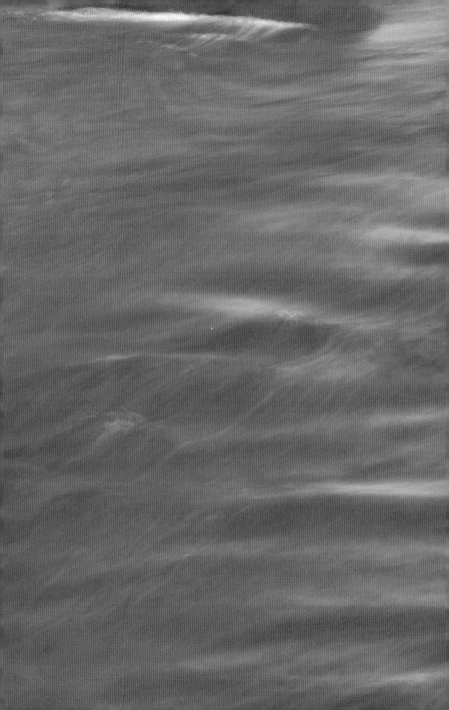

生命の火

Ashes to ashes

電気やガスのコンロしか
知らなければ
火鉢の中で真っ黒な炭に
ぽっと紅く火が点る瞬間の
あの美しさはわからない
炭火と鉄瓶のお湯のまろやかさ
火鉢で焼いたお餅の香ばしさ

火と聞いて連想するのは
ぱちぱちとはぜる音霊の調べ
木炭が静かに白く燃えつきて
灰となり

その灰が次の新たな炭を熾し
火を育むための
ゆりかごとなっていく
その様子はまるで
目の前で繰り広げられる
生命の連鎖のように美しい

人生の布

Weaving of Life

人の一生は
大きな一枚の布を
織り上げていく道のり
時間の縦糸に
一日また一日と
横糸を通し
一本ずつ重ねていく
毎日ただひたすら同じ横糸を

通し続けるだけの人生もあれば

糸の色や素材を変えて

布に好きな模様や

絵を描きあげていく人生もあります

いずれにせよ大切なのは

ときどき作業の手を休めて

二歩三歩、ときには十歩二十歩と

後ろに下がって

ゆっくりと布全体を眺めて

そのでき栄えを

確かめること

ひとつ現実のはたおりと違うのは

布の完成がいつになるか

それどころか

完成できるのかどうかさえも

判らないこと

それでも私たちは毎日コツコツと

はたおりを続けていくのです

意識の循環

Endless Space Odyssey

生命盛る夏が終わり
静寂の秋が過ぎ
やがて死の冬を迎え
そして春になると聞こえてくる
新たな生命の息吹

私たちの体内でも
ほんの一瞬も止まることなく
生と死の循環が続いています

原子のレベルから肉体を見れば
5年前のあなたといまのあなたは
まったくの別人

私であるというアイデンティティ
私は他の誰でもなく
変わらないのは意識だけ

私たちの肉体に宿っていた意識（魂）は
いずれ蒸気の粒子のようになって
風に運ばれ
雨にさらされ
大地に降り注がれて

地下の水脈に沿って流れていきます
命はその流れる水に転写されながら
長い歳月を経て再び海に還ります
意識（魂）は宇宙の広大な海原から
したたり落ちたのち
やがて上昇しながら
果てしない宇宙の旅を続けていくのです
あなたとは意識そのもの
私も意識そのもの

希望の寿命

Dedicated Seeker

人の歓びや幸せに共感できるのは
その人の中に純粋な心を見たとき
感動はそこから生まれる

猜疑心や嫉妬心は
本当の感動をもたらしません

在るべき場所を求めて進む
ひたむきな探求者の姿は

人々に感動を与えます

手探りで進む真っ暗な世界

希望の光は

彼らの足元を照らしてくれるでしょう

でもその光の寿命は

そう長くはありません

希望の光を燃やし続けるには

なにがあっても前に進み続ける覚悟

そしてなにより勇気が必要です

勇気を出して

Run-up to cross the wall

〈ゆとり〉はどうすれば生まれるのでしょう

答えはきわめてシンプルです

ゆとりをもたずたくさん動くこと

動けるうちに心も体もフルに活動させることです

そうすればいつかその継続が血肉となり智恵となって

成功をもたらしてくれるはず

事を成してこそ自信も持てます

自信がつけば乗り越える力が身に付きます

そこに〈ゆとり〉が生まれます

それでも乗り越えられないときは

他人や環境のせいにしてはいけません

勇気を出していったん後ろに下がり

そして再び走り出しましょう

壁を乗り越えるには

助走が必要なのです

靴と小石

靴の中の小石のように

他人から見れば取るに足らない

小さなことでも

自分にとっては小さくない

そういうことはよくあります

そんな〈小石〉ひとつのせいで

毎日が色あせてしまうのは

あまりにも馬鹿らしい

どんなに急いでいたとしても

そこでいったん歩みを止めて

少しくらい時間はかかっても

靴を脱いで逆さに振って

さっさと小石を

捨ててしまいましょう

そのほうがけっきょく早く

目的地に着けるのです

しかも快適に

想像する旅

A magic carpet called imagination

生きているということは
動いているということ
動いているから生きていける
生きているから心も動き
心が動くから感情が生まれ
その感情がまた人を動かす
感情は感情を動かし
新たな人の動きを
作り出す

人が動くことから旅は始まる

旅の目的は

ここではないどこかへ行くこと

それは環境を変え

自分を変えるため

けれども人は

動かなくても旅はできる

想像力という名の

魔法のじゅうたんに乗って

どこにでも自由に飛んで行けるから

あとがき

　子供の頃、家の近所の松林に遊びに行くことが私の何よりの楽しみだった。木登りするには小さ過ぎて枝に手の届かない私の手を、年上の男の子たちが引っ張り上げてくれる。ゴワゴワとした鱗のような樹皮の感触。あたりに漂う松の清々しい緑の香りを胸いっぱいに吸い込みながら、私は龍神の背中にまたがって空を飛ぶ自分を想像した。

　松林の前に広がる浜辺に出れば必ず貝殻を探した。

　直射日光から頭を守るためにと、母から常にかぶっているよう厳命されていた帽子も、けっきょく最後は珍しい貝殻や松毬を入れるための容れ物と化した。

　私にとっては松林も浜辺も新しい発見のための宝庫であり聖地であった。

　私に人一倍強い好奇心と冒険心を植え付けたのは父だった。

　しつけに厳しかった母とは対象的に、破天荒で旅好きの父は、私が小学校に上がる前から私に天文学の本を与え、星座の位置を教え、そして世界の広さを教えてくれた。だから今でも一日中空を眺めていてもまったく飽きることがない。

　この本は、そんな私が子どもの頃から現在にいたるまで、自分を取り囲む自然の中を歩きながら、泳ぎながら、立ち止まりながら、ときに寝転がりながら考えたことを文章に書

き留めたものをまとめたものだ。

ところで私には5つ年下の弟がいる。私と違って大人しい性分。人に威張るということをしない。姉の私からみれば、それが凄くうらやましい。だって私はすぐ威張るから。威張っても良いことなんて一つもないのについつい威張る。

だけど彼と私はとても仲がいい。両親のおかげだ。私たち姉弟に財産の類をいっさい遺さない代わりに、たくさんの教育とさまざまな経験を与えてくれた。だからいわゆる兄弟間での骨肉の争いなどといったものとは無縁でいられる。

私も自分の子供たちにはそうしようと考えている。自立する力のみを与え、あとは子どもたちが自分で自分自身の人生を歩めばいい。

父が他界してから随分と経ったいまだから言えることがある。

生前、父とはなにかとぶつかってきたけれど、死んだらとたんに父が恋しくなった。嫌いだったあんなところこんなところが何よりも愛おしく感じる。母がなぜ父を心の底から愛していたのかいまになって少しだけわかるような気がする。

私の中に父が生きていて、母が生きていて、そしてご先祖さまたちも生きている——そう思える自分が好きだ。

「冒険するために生きているんだ」って声を大にして空に向かって叫びたい。

約束された人生なんて信じない！

そうそう、私には毎日意識していることがある。

人生で起きることは全て必然だというけれど、私はそう思わない。この世界は〈偶然〉

と〈必然〉の掛け合わせで成り立っていて、たまたま起きた〈偶然〉にどう意味をもたせ

るか、だと思っている。大きな不運に見舞われて失意のどん底にいる人に、それも必然だ

などとはとても言えない。すべてが運命で決まっているなんて、考えただけで面白くない！

人間は〈偶然〉を〈必然〉に変える自由をもっている。運命も自由意志でいくらでも変え

られるはずだ。

人生では〈偶然〉と〈必然〉が必ず背中合わせで存在していて、あることが現象として

あらわれた時にどう意味づけをし、どう解釈をするのか。それが大事だと思う。

だから私は予め定まった運命に身をゆだねるなどということはしたくない。

私は死ぬまで動きたいし、働き続けたい。なぜなら単純に働けるというのはすごく幸せ

なことだからだ。

職業に貴賤はないけれど、生き方には貴賤はある。

卑しい生き方は魂を腐らせる——。

220

母がいつも口癖のように言う言葉だ。だから誤解を恐れずに言うならば私は私を一番信用している。かなり自惚れも入っているのだけれどそう思わなければやっていけない。だからこの本にも私はすべて心の根っこから思っていることを書いたつもりだ。

なにかふとした折に、気が向いたときに、どこからでもいいのでページをめくって目を通して、なにか感じていただければ筆者としてこれ以上の幸せはありません。

最後になりましたが、この私の本のために本当に素晴らしい写真の数々を撮ってくださった写真家の館野二朗さん、アイデアに満ちた最高の装丁をほどこしていただいたスタジオギブの山岡茂さん、山本雅一さん、そして出版のきっかけと機会を与えてくださった飯塚書店の飯塚行男社長、プロデューサーの白崎博史さん、本当にお世話になりました。

誰ひとり欠けてもこの本は創れませんでした。心から感謝しています。

令和四年九月吉日

藤山邦子

著者プロフィール

藤山邦子（ふじやま くにこ）

駐日サンマリノ共和国大使館特別顧問
聖アガタ騎士団 Cavaliere（日本人女性初の叙勲）
株式会社en art&design 代表取締役会長
株式会社きたやま取締役副社長
平成元年 英ヴァージンアトランティック航空第一期生クルー
に採用されアッパークラス担当。
平成27年3月27日 伊勢神宮 神社本庁宮司 北白川道久氏よ
り感謝状授与。
令和2年年12 月23 日 照国神社宮司島津修久氏より感謝状
授与。
令和3年4 月サンマリノ共和国特命全権大使マンリオ・カデ
ロ駐日157ヵ国駐日外交団長とともに華厳宗総裁で東大寺
別当（第222 世・第223 世）の狹川普文氏を公式表敬訪問。
スポーツ、芸術、政治など幅広い分野で要人や海外との交
流が多く、民間外交に従事しており、「より良い世界を作る」
というタイトルで「グローカル」をテーマにオンラインも含め
様々な会議を積極的に開催している。

観測者の杜
かんそくしゃのもり

2022 年 11 月 1 日　初版第 1 刷発行

著　者	藤山　邦子	
写　真	館野　二朗	
編　集	白崎　博史	
装幀・組版	スタジオ・ギブ	
発行者	飯塚　行男	
発行所	株式会社飯塚書店	
	http://izbooks.co.jp	
	〒 112-0002	
	東京都文京区小石川 5-16-4	
	TEL03-3815-3805	
	iizuka@izbooks.co.jp	
印刷・製本	シナノパブリッシングプレス	

The Grove
of
the Observer
Kuniko FUJIYAMA

The babbling of the brook, the whistling of the breeze between the trees of the forest

The shimmering of the flora in the rays gushing down through the trees, the coming and going of the waves on the seashore

In the meadow, the fluttering of butterflies and birds, the downpour of the rain

From immemorial age man has learned from the endless rhythms of nature

From the endless knowledge, on and on we have learned.

Beginning of the Beginning

Why is it that we are alive.
Subatomic particles form atoms,
atoms gather to form molecules,
and molecules combine in various
ways to form the cells, tissues,
and organs of living things.
At every level, new properties
are being created which are not
simply the sum of their parts.
The hierarchical structure in
which smaller things shape
larger things and create other
new properties may be the basic
principle that forms our world.
And if we follow the hierarchy,
the beginning of "existence"
comes down to "one."
If our lives have meaning, then
the "one" also has meaning.
In other words, everything has
meaning.
It all has meaning !
And with those words, I would
like to begin this book.

Messages from The Forest
Something you need

While walking in the forest
As the breeze tingles the tip of your nose
Or perhaps while wind is stagnant

That scent begins to bloom
And you notice things
The sweet and sour aroma of ripe fruit
And that's when you're hungry
When your heart is full
It's the freshness of the flowers
When it's the scent of the water
Then your throat is dry
Your ears
Are yearning for the babble of the brook
In such a way
In the many forms of the forest
Messages are sent
That which you need
It will tell you

The Heavens
Made in heaven

Riding in a little boat
Coming down a long river
Partway through there may be good currents
And bad currents, perhaps
When the flow is disrupted
Be not caught up in the obstacle of it
Watch yourself from the sky above
The greatness beyond oneself
Contemplate existence
There is no good or bad in nature
The only truth that can be said
Is to follow the voice of your heart
That one should be willing to "Live Higher"
Live in a way that does not shame the heavens
In that way it can be overcome
For the Heavens
Have made the world in this way

The Harmony of the Rainbow
Gift from the universe

A rainbow appears in the sky after the rains
Like a harmonic chord from the clouds

That gift from the beyond
Is on the earth somewhere every day
Someone is there, looking up at a rainbow
The rainbow is a symbol of harmony

Birds singing together
Flattering harmony
And we
Might gently inspire one another so
How wonderful that could be

The Sea and The Land
Waiting for the sunrise

A beach at dawn
The breath of the cascading waves
My breath in unison, I walk barefoot
The crisp crunch of the sand
Blends with the sound of the waves
And becomes one rhythm
Crunchcrunchwhoosh
Crunchcrunchwhoosh
In the deep blue sky
Glittering stars
And the horizon, beyond and below
As if drawn in a brushstroke
The gradation of morning light
I stop in my tracks
Quietly lay my body down
Close my eyes
And listen to the voice
It's important to listen with one's whole body
And all the cells within the body
Turn every last one into an ear drum
The earth and sea meet
The rhythm of the beautiful, elegant words
You can perk your ears
While waiting for the day to break

Sanzui / Defining water
Shape of water

Through the benevolence of light and wind
The source of life has been protected
Over the course of many moons
In all its vicissitudes
Liquid, gas, and solid
Repetition of the trifecta of change
Water is the foundation of life
The rays of the sun birth dewdrops
Become mist
Bringing the bounty of prosperity to the earth

Water cleanses the great earth

Rinse, purify, and hydrate

Our sweat and tears, as well
All return to the waters

Returning through the rivers to the ocean

Water is the source of all

The mysterious definition

Flower Unnamed
As it is in the field

The flower that blooms in the fields
Plucked
Rather than displayed in a vase
The form it took on the field
Is far more beautiful
While in The Forest
From the bottom of my heart
There is a moment I have felt so
You need not look up its name right away
With "beautiful," "lovely," or "sweet"
And such words
Without modification
Just the way it is
We can enjoy the flowers as they are

All Things Are My Teacher
All that which exists in the world
There is meaning in it all
There is something to be learned from it all
Simply by remembering that
Tomorrow's world
Will show us an entirely
New face

When the Noise of the Heart is Gone
A moment of stillness

When pondering a decision
So that you may hear the voice of your heart
You close your eyes
You open your ears
Even so, now and then
It does not always go well
This is the idle stream of consciousness
It is the noise of the heart
When we listen to the radio
If you fail to match the frequency
You hear only static
At such times
Walk in the forest
The crunch of footsteps on dry leaves
The voices of the birds and the bugs
The whistling of the wind through the trees
In the distance, the roar of the sea
While immersing in the sound of the forest
A sudden overwhelming calm of the heart
Arrives for a moment
This is nature's
Noise Cancelling System

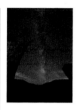

The Observer of the Space Forest
Where beauty is expressed

In the deep, deep forest of space
We observe the place of stars turned trees
The equilibrium of distance from star to star
The gathering, glittering rivers and clouds
Powdery light glistening far away
Where beauty manifests
Distant memories, floating there
To love and be loved
The expression of the celestial
Flattering one another
Being flattered in turn
And for the greater existence
Awe and desire
Yearning for mysticism
The subliminal
Beauty of Form

Waves of Tears
Whispers from the Deep

Repeating over the sand
Rumbling low
Silver waves lap at the shore
The sound of the waves
Whispers from the distant deep
Like witchy incantations
The concept of time
Is put in doubt
The sight before one's eyes
Is but the boundary between sea and land

Trying to dredge up the land
The sounds of phantasmagoric sands
With the power of the wind and the sea combined
From beyond the exponential repetition of time
It calls to us
Expanding our imagination
The path of legends weaving time and space
Bringing nostalgia to mind
That which the silver waves have made
Are wrought by the innumerable flow of tears

Two Forests
Forest full of wonders

Waking early in the morning
Walking in the forest
Asked by my two sons,
"How was the forest?"
And their mother responds,
"Insects here, there and everywhere…"
The eldest drops his shoulders, disappointed
But the second son's expression glows
That there were many birds and insects
That many lovely flowers bloomed
That I slipped and almost fell on the moss
He would like to talk forever
To the eldest it's a "forest full of insects"
To the youngest "a forest full of wonder"
Between the two of them
It became a meaningful morning to me
Which was it, I wonder
Blocked by a single "loathing" or "aversion"
Nothing can be seen beyond
It seems like such a waste

Waves of Emotion
Stand up again

With the disturbing rumblings of the sea
Great waves come crashing in
Try not to be swept away
Desperately resisting footholds
A pebbly torrent of waves
Relentless scraping
Still, for you
The pain is tolerable
No matter the wave
One day, you will surely pull through
Of this you are certain
And if you still can't stand it
There is always the ocean into which you can dive
The one thing you must always keep
No matter how muddy the waters
Your eyes must always stay open
You must not turn your sight from yourself
In that way
When the tide abates
All at once, you will be able to stand again

Take a Deep Breath
Nature has the answer

When we are born into this world
The first thing we do
Is to breathe
This is why "to live"
Is "to breathe"
It looks simple
But the process is complex
It's not just respiration
Life is being preserved
Our bodies are being built
Millions of cells are repeating
Tens, hundreds of thousands of times per second
A product of chemical reactions
Of this process
We humans know little
Our bodies – all of nature
From the birth of this world
The answers are all known
Even in the midst of sinking in sorrow
Every day inside your own body
A trillion cells die
The same number are born
Let us not forget this miracle while we live
Now, take a deep breath!

True Strength
The strength nature demands

Growing and spreading with pride
The large tree stretching its leafy branches
Unable to withstand the storms and blizzards
Finally broke, and fell
On the other hand, even faint breezes
Makes it shiver and sway unsteadily
Willows don't fall under a little wind or snow
Nature demands true strength
A single-minded nature about all things
That we face head-on
Rather than rigidity
Against hardship and tribulation
Become flexible and overcome
There is more nobility in the pliable
And thus stronger people are kind

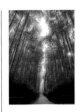

An Everyday Day
Turn off the autopilot

My usual route for a walk
I walk deep in thought
And then I realize I am already in front of my house
My usual route to work
I walk along without consideration
When I look up
I'm already in front of my office
I wonder why this is
Every day feels new
A childhood full of curiosity
I gradually grew older
Every new day brought by the sun
Became "just another day"
A pile of routine tasks
Seeing, hearing, talking, smiling, laughing on cue
Walking, eating, breathing
Both work and locking up the house
All of living is done unconsciously
Left to the "autopilot"
We trace our own footsteps
We don't realise we are tracing lives
Those countless footsteps without realizing
Become deep ruts
We move along in the ruts
Let's stop a moment
Disengage the autopilot
Now, where's your switch?

The Shape of Love
Love over time

Consider dogs and cats, sheep and horses, pigs and ducks
Transcending their species, they play
They sympathize and help one another
How very heartwarming
Or lions and zebras together, perhaps
Usually the eater and the eaten
I am deeply moved

On the battlefield where lives are taken
Enemy soldiers holding hands
Who have been enemies for years
These countries' people, embracing one another
When the Berlin Wall crumbled
I saw that moment
People all over the world wept
Because of the depth
Of the love they felt
What about man and woman
Transcending gender, the man and the woman
Can be tied together by love
But for that to happen
Men and women should not simply gaze at one another
But have the same soul
Must speak of the same star
To gaze so is to make the decision
The color of romance fades with time
But the hue of true love deepens with time

The Scent of Memory
Memories in the wind

Now and then
A very nostalgic smell
Tickles your nostrils
I stop there unconsciously
And let my nose sniff
It was a long time ago
When I played as a child
The grass in the sun
The sandbox in the park
A hovel of old trees
What was the scent
I try to remember
I can't right away
But surely one day
The wind will bring it back
Along with a distant memory

Like the Verdure
For a more fruitful life

For those living on earth
When wrapped in the universe
The loneliness of existence is healed
Breathing in the whole

Of all the things that live on earth

The life that best embodies the heavenly movements
Are the plants
As beings living on this earth
If we could look to the heavens like the plants
Turning our hearts thither
Life could be more fruitful
Yet we humans try to keep a distance from nature
Observing through a monitor
How sad that it becomes a mere concept

The Christmas Tree in the Forest
Harmony of life form

Under a full sky of stars
Gazing up at the night from inside the forest
Through the leaves and branches of the trees
The twinkling of stars
Just like a Christmas tree
Whenever I see this I am convinced
In this universe, true isolation
Exists nowhere
And so it is......
All matter in the universe
Began as one
Our physical bodies, too
Stars billions of light years away, too
All from the same place
Born at the same time
From subatomic particles
The trillions of cells of our bodies
Are connected in a network
In harmony as one living organism
And so they continue to exist
Because all the cells, with the same genes
Are connected
And the innumerable stars in the universe
And us, too
From the moment this world was born
We are all connected by a single chain
Called subatomic particles

Sharing Luck
Seeds of fortune

When I went to the forest
I ended up with a bounty of nuts
I gathered a basket full
Too many for one person to eat
What would you do
Share with your friends and neighbors?
Or eat them by yourself until you get sick?
Most people probably
Would choose <to share> with others
Rather than eating in secret alone
It feels better to please everyone
What if they were seeds of good fortune
Could you share those like nuts
Whether you could really capture good luck or not
Would be all about the nuts
In the words of a great writer
Lady Luck favors those who are kind
And who can share their fortune
The luck that came to you
Must be given generously to others
You will miss out on fortune if you keep it all for yourself
The seeds of fortune that you shared one day
May sprout and once again
Come back to you once more
But don't count on it
Keep your heart high and unburdened
That is the key to everything

The Joy of Life
Joy of life

What is always present within us
Resides there always
The deepest existence
The highest will
So that we may touch them
We must feel the joy of life

We must love nature

The sound of dragonfly wings
Drifting powder of butterflies
Fuzz on a morning glory
The whispering of stars

Listen carefully, squint your eyes
Savor it fully
All the senses in your body
Keep on polishing them with vigor

In this way experience all senses fully
Not just pretending to live for "the sake of living"
Not just being alive

Cloud
Symbol of the Universe

Water that echoes the primordial wave
Roaring with the lapping
Nurturing life
Waves are the dance of roots
Swirling in opposite directions
Rising to the heavens
Becoming clouds

They become a sign of the sky

People would read the signs above
Clouds, present with the birth of the earth

The wake of a grand mass of energy
A symbol of the universe

The Gift of the Rhinoceros Beetle
Just want to help, so I do.

He appeared in last night's rain
In a puddle on a stump
Drowning
I found a rhinoceros beetle
I gently picked him up with my fingers
Let him grab onto a tree branch nearby
The beetle remained for a moment
As if grooming his hair
After shaking off his legs
Of course
Without a word of thanks
Nor did he bid farewell
He flew off somewhere
That's all there was to it

If you see someone in trouble before you
Always as such
I wish I could help them
Just to help them if I could
That's enough
You made me realise this
Thank you, rhinoceros beetle

Prayer for Life
Watch over our children

Spirits of Thunder, Water and Fire
Ancestors beyond
May our hearts
Be awakened to tolerance and harmony

Sun, moon and stars
Spirits of the sea, the forest, the air, and the earth
Watch over our descendants

When we offer the prayer of life
To the great universe and nature
When we kneel and bow down
Towards the light of life
And open
To the blessings and cycle of grace
We give thanks

Wind and the Bicycle
Leaves away from branches

Riding a bicycle along the river road
The breeze is a headwind
My cheeks are burning
The scent of spring caresses
Hurry, hurry
The wind picks up
I lean forward into it
Putting strength into my pedaling legs

The way home
Speeding up
I'm riding so fast
And yet the wind
Seems to have stopped

That's where you learn
People are quick to recognize a headwind
But when a tailwind is pushing them
It's hard to notice
And I see the crossing glide
Of the fallen leaves, and think
For the leaves parted from the branches
There is no headwind
Nor tailwind

The Many Moons
Read the Moon

Most people today
Know the moon affects the earth
But this knowledge
Has been procured by science

The ancients in the past
Read the moon like a calendar
Not only as a guide
But an object of reverential worship
Even without knowledge of astronomy or physics
The mystical power of the moon
Bestowed by Mother Nature
Could be felt reverberating in the soul

Consider us living in the modern age
Those with that sensitivity
How few they must be
Relinquish, a moment, the knowledge of the mind
Ponder the ancients
The moon for what it is
The celestial bodies
The nature
Feel it

Human Magnetism
Magnetic fields of human

A compass is
A necessity when walking in a deep forest
When I was a child I learned in school
That the earth is a big magnet
Not like a permanent bar magnet
But an electromagnet
The core at the center of the earth
Melted iron and other metals
By the currents generated during convection
A magnetic field is formed

And so are we humans
Colliding and melting into one another
All the while, convecting
Creating our own magnetic fields
Thanks to this field
The earth and its inhabitants
From solar winds and strong ultraviolet rays
We are protected, it is said

The fields we create are like that too
I would like to think

To Sky, To Land, To Man
Pray to the Stars

Those who try, to one's own will
Manipulate others
Are the furthest from freedom
A free person
Does not try
To control others
It is because he is crippled
That he tries to move someone else

To make things happen

How pointless

Freedom is, for one's own sake
To take initiative

Not take advantage of or cause society trouble
Walking with solemnity
One's own path
This is the beauty of humanity
Finally, we fold our hands
Letting the sun shine on us
Purify
Allow your tired body and soul
To be cleansed under the moonlit night

Offer your sincere prayers to the stars
Prayers that have gone on for ten thousand years
To heaven, to earth, to man
May it reach them all

Perfect Existence
Integrity from Within

We are all born naked
We are born with nothing
The same as all other animals
The only difference is how humans "own"
Food, clothing, shelter, transportation, ornament...
More than we could ever hold alone
We try to gain possessions and assets
And fame, and status
Things without substance

Animals own nothing
And live their entire lives as such
From the moment they are born
Because they have everything
In other words they are perfect beings

It could be true of human beings
Even if you think you have nothing
We have a little universe inside of us
We have "perfection"
Yet we always think we're missing something
That's why we want this and that
But that doesn't mean what we have
Should be a source of shame
Because a person

Can give

The Tomorrow Self
Me tomorrow

Just as we look at the past from the present
Look back and see the present from the future

The tomorrow Now
Today's Self
I wonder how it will look

I wonder how I as a child
Would think when looking
At me now

I have shaped myself into who I am today
Reconsidering my habits and viewpoints
I have tried to break out of my mold and shell

(After all, I Am…)

Of all the creatures on earth
Only humans think that way
Any living thing
Is simply fulfilling the life
It is given

It's quite beautiful and precious

Harmonious Colors
Wavelength of rainbow

The forest in the autumn
Is painted with many colors
Though we simply say "autumn leaves"
Each and every leaf differs in shade

So are people's personalities and charms
We say, "ten people, ten colors"
Expression in an allegory of colors
Different colored faces
Different colored hair
The reason colors look different
Is the different wavelengths
Of being on the same wavelength
Or not
It is often said
"It would be easier if we
were on the same wavelength"
In many ways
But that's not how the world spins
Though someone may not be on your wavelength
You begin to accept it as you go along together
Surely that is where harmony is born

It is because rainbows are made of many wavelengths
That they are beautiful

Magnifying Glass of Happiness
Treasures on the Roadside

Whenever I go out for a walk
I always take a magnifying glass with me
Flowers and grass I find along the way
Fallen on the roadside
A pebble or a shell
Dragonfly wings
Catching my attention
Anything at hand
Bring my magnifying glass close
Carefully see, look, watch

Spreading beyond the Convex Lens
What you thought you knew but didn't
A world of surprise and excitement
When you find it
You feel you've gained something
Such happiness
You don't need a real magnifying glass
Anywhere and everywhere
Seeds of happiness are scattered
We all have them in our hearts
Search with a magnifying glass of happiness

Illusions of Happiness
Healing of the Earth

Earthquakes, typhoons, floods, blizzards
People call them disasters
But the earth repairs itself
Has the power to heal itself

Much of what is destroyed is man-made
Man-made objects invite further destruction
Layer after layer of concrete
Mountains, rivers, and beaches
Life having been squeezed out
Losing their place
With no way to resist
They quietly perish

The balance of dark and light that generates all
That governs the gradation of shadows

The unseen majesty of heavenly motion
Forgetting the awe of it
If one were to fulfill one's own desires
What could be gained is but
An emotionless illusion of happiness
It never lasts long

We all desire to be happy
But for whom
The time has come for us to ask ourselves

The Dance of Life
Seize the day

Gazing at the stars on a sandy beach
Embraced in the bosom of a forest dripping with green
Pondering the depth of the sea and the height of the sky
I always feel
That science and mythology
Are not inconsistent
Nor are they contradictory
But complementary of each other

That which has been given to human beings
Absolute freedom is
The freedom to imagine
No one can take that power away from us
That we can use it to the fullest
Allows us men to find "the Real"

A scientist once said
There are only two ways to live life
One is to live as if nothing is a miracle
The other is to live as if everything is a miracle

From the perspective of the history of the universe
Even if each individual's life is but a moment
It is a continuous chain of living
Eternity, into a great river
Shall continue to expand
As a drop of water created the sea
Each one of us is in the midst of this miracle
Swinging in the dance of life
Perhaps that is what it means to "live in the moment"

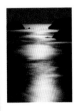

Beautiful Darkness
Joy of being here and now

To be emotionally moved is like
Every adjective evaporating
The head stops still
While the heart begins to move

It's not only the starry night
That is beautiful

Everything is black
As if painted over
The pitch darkness is beautiful
The clouds floating in the sky
And the plants shivering in the wind
I can't see them
I only feel their presence

The sound of waves washing the beach
Of being here and now
Teaches me of joy

Wonder of the Sprout
Finding hidden beauty

The sharing of joy is
The bond of perception
Touching the hearts of many
True treasure
The moment you think it's only for you
It loses its luster

In nature
The hidden beauty
Must be found
To be given
Let the days of waiting and hoping
Be put to an end

A heart that can be emotionally touched
Is not something that can be learned
A little sprout of "?" that floats up in your heart
To be nurtured with care

Path of Hope
Shadows on the water's bottom

As if running away
The days which have gone by
The future which comes racing in
All in one space
Quietly overlapping
At the entrance to the new dimension of the Now

I lean over the swaying waves
Overlooking my own shadow reflected in the depths

With unwavering honesty
Supple thinking

And a dash of the ego blended in
I want to continue to choose the path of hope

Again Tomorrow
If only I could remember

To me, the past
Separate from the time axis
Spatially intertwining and expanding
A vignette of the five senses

How I've mistreated you in the past
There is no need to bring it up again now
Still, the experience of
Overcoming much pain and suffering
Not solely my own
But that of family and friends
If it could mean even a little respite for the heart
There could be nothing happier
The body will decay one day
But if we could leave our memories behind

Those living life to the fullest against the backdrop of pain
The innocent voices of children laughing

The scent of brine across the surface of the deep azure sea
The endless freshness of the blue sky
The vivacity of flora that celebrate life
I enshrine them in my heart

I will see you again tomorrow

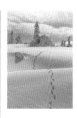

With Your Own Legs
Go your own way

The path that everyone walks
Is a new road for each of us
There are several forks in the road
Whichever fate you choose
The first step is
Exploratory
But if you still feel lost
When it won't go away
As if walking in the shoal of a river
Take off your shoes
And tread on barefoot
Then touch the wind
Catch the current
Look up to the sky and check the place of the stars

See your own path to the end
Walking on your own feet
When you've made up your mind
You'll be unburdened
From envying others
And from being envied
You should able to walk free

The Universe Within
Invisible light

A dark forest not even moonlight can enter
While the animals within are busy scurrying
We humans cannot move without light
Since we can perceive
Only Visible Light

In the same way, there are things in this universe
That the human eye cannot see, unexplained
As innumerable as the stars

It can only be described a miracle
An exquisite equilibrium beyond human understanding

The earth and life on it
We must keep this in our hearts now
As you go about your day to day
In your work and in personal life
When something is not going well
Depart a moment from words and logic
Quietly ponder the universe within
Such time of introspection
May be necessary perhaps

Doubt Yourself
It's Magic !

The magician on stage
Selects a member of the audience
The magic trick he is to perform
Is about to be revealed
A very common scene
In such a situation, the magician chooses
One who looks stubborn and deeply doubtful
"I believe only what I see with my own eyes"
That type of person
A man of great perception
But missing one thing
Could it be, only what you want to see
Is all you see
Perhaps you even doubt yourself
Not believing though you do see

Seeing comes from believing
The more strongly they believe
That they won't be fooled
The more gullible they are
This is said because it happens
It is when you think, "I see!"
That you should rub your eyes and look more closely

Omen
Always be by your side

We are born into this world
Stand up on our own feet
Before we begin to walk
We stumble many times
And fall
They always reach out their hand to you
And help you up
Someone nearby to help you
So that you may learn, perhaps

When having a major setback
Maybe unable to rise again
Even when you feel like so
There is someone there to help you
Stars and Potential that gathers to support you

Sometimes
With the smallest of provocations or signs
It begins
To notice, or not to notice
That small difference
Determines the rest of our lives

Resonance
Firm magnetic field

For a newborn baby
The world is its mother's arms

And from there, day by day
Little by little
The world, outwardly
Expands
As the world expands
Consciousness expands
Imagination expands

That is why

Others' feelings resonate
And can be empathized with

Resonance creates a magnetic field
That makes it stronger
From that magnetic field
All things arise
Resonance can be positive
Or negative

Even those who do evil
Resonate with each other
We must not forget this
Do not be disturbed
By the words and deeds of others
Create a strong magnetic field

Connected
God is looking over you

Contribution to Humanity
Service to the Earth

"That's a big deal."
You may think

However......
It is important to keep wondering
About the origin and essence of things

You are always connected to a higher will
Being watched by The Heavens
Always keep this in the back of your mind

That you are connected to the source of all life
Chained to it
Picture in your heart
No matter how far away you are
We are a blessing, and a blessed existence

A Free Soul
Feelings of freedom

When touched by magnificent vibrations
We lose our words
And become pure spirit

Active cells
Their cycle of life and death
The vibrations of the spirit and the body overlap

To the highest level of awareness
Resonance occurs

Without logical judgement
No limitation of consciousness
Feeling true freedom in the depths of the soul
Overflowing with awe

What Mode are You In Now ?
Switching operation buttons

Appliances have "energy saving mode"
Or "silent mode"
Just as there are many modes of functionality
We humans, too, have many modes
Cynic Mode, Resentment Mode, Anger Mode
When you made mistakes in the past
When you didn't get the result you wanted
Remember carefully
What mode you were in at that time
Frustrated Mode, Jaded Mode, Weak Mode
Now that you know it
Press the mode switch button
If you failed in Frustrated Mode, go to Cool Mode
From Resentment Mode to Calm Mode
If you don't know what you're doing
Reset to Neutral
And then flip the switch
On again
Switch modes

Information War
Open your mind

Compassion
Taking into account the feelings of others
It's very simple
Bargaining is
Hiding yourself
So that you may read the other's mind
And use it
In other words, information warfare
It's complicated and tedious
That's why it's so tiring
Work, love and socializing

In the truest sense
What brings people closer together
It is not the false information
Exchanged on social networking
Others are Others, You are You
Facebook, Twitter, Instagram.....
Close your smartphone browser
Open your heart
To the people you are with now

The Nature of Anxiety
Don't be afraid to get hurt

Childhood memories
Waiting in line for the jab
Waiting for my turn
(I wonder if it hurts)
(What if it hurts)
My heart is pounding with anxiety
But once the shot is over
Even if it hurts a little bit
My heart feels much lighter
I didn't need to worry so much
That's how I feel

The fear of getting hurt
Is much more painful than actually being hurt
Because "fear" lasts much longer
Than "pain"
It's more damaging to the heart

If you have time to be afraid
With a battle cry
Take a step forward
If you get hurt, you get hurt
That's okay
You will find the remedy
Please remember
There is no cure for "painful anxiety"

The True Self
What nature does without knowing it

The stains we unwittingly accumulate

Nature silently purifies

The natural Self -- The true Self
So that it may be regained
Within yourself you must recognize
Lies, deceit, hubris, hatred, and mistrust
One can never be rid of them
Because they are also nature
We must not turn our eyes away from "existence"
When we reflect on our shortcomings
Only can our true nature
And our true self be reclaimed

So that you may be your True Self
Enjoy your true self

Shiny dishes
Shiny shoes
Shiny windows
Shiny smiles
No matter what it is
Being shiny is a good state
Everyday life is that way
It's better to sparkle
That goes without saying
Polish away the grime that sticks to you
Until your true self is revealed

To be more like your true self
You have to overcome who you are now

But beware of over-polishing
You'll get tired
And you will wear yourself out
Self-polish in moderation

Vessels of Life
Steady or free?

Two ships on the ocean
One is a large passenger ship
Life on this stable ship is comfortable
The other is a small ship
Minimal equipment on board
Shaking like leaves on a tree
Fishing for food every day

However a voyage has emergencies
Like a sudden appearance
Of a huge iceberg
Only a small ship can turn nimbly
A large ship cannot quickly change course
Or a big storm may suddenly arise
Emergency evacuation to the nearest port
In such a case
The small ship can enter any port
But the large ship cannot

Take the stability of a big ship
Or the freedom of a small ship
It is not a matter of vanity or worldliness
It is your heart that decides
There is no right answer in life

Living the Whole
Accept differences

Strong people, weak people, bright people, dull people
Stubborn people, flexible people
Lively people, meek people
Gentle people, mean people......
It is natural that there are all kinds in the world
That's what makes a society work
Consider a building that looks solid itself
From rubber to steel
Materials of various properties are used
Only then can it maintain its solidity

Only when opposites exist
Can the Whole exist
The existence of what is contrary to oneself
As foreign or alien
Instead of elimination or rejection
By accepting them
It's possible to live as a Whole

Courage to return
Back to the Beginning

A man walks on the sand
His steps are slow and heavy
When he set out
The landmarks visible
Are no longer such
Where is he going
Is he getting closer to his goal
Or moving away
He knows not even that

What he should do is
Climb to the top of the hill
Where he can see across the desert
And find the target once more
And if he still can't find it
He must garner courage
Follow his own footsteps
Back to the place
Where he can see his goal
And take a new step again

Fire of Life
Ashes to ashes

If you know only electric or gas stoves
You will never know the beauty
Of the moment, the burst
When the pitch black coals in the hearth are lit red
The mellowness of the charcoal
The simmer of water in the iron kettle
The aroma of rice cakes roasted on a brazier

When I hear the word "fire" I think of
The crackles and flutters of the spirit
Charcoal quietly burning down to white
Turning to ash

The ashes make new charcoal
To nurture the next fire
Turning into a cradle
The scene is in all ways
Spreading before your eyes
Beautiful like a chain of life

The Cloth of Life
Weaving of Life

A person's life
A large piece of cloth
The path of weaving it
On the warped thread of time
Day by day
Weft threads are woven
Growing one by one
The same weft thread day after day
Defines some lives
Or change the color or material
Weave in your favorite pattern
Drawing a picture in some lives

In any case it's important
Sometimes you must rest your hands
Take two or three, sometimes ten or twenty
Steps backwards
Gaze at the cloth slowly as a whole
How well it turned out
To be sure

Where it differs from a real weaver
Is when the cloth is finished
To the contrary
Whether mine will ever be finished
I know not
But day in and day out
I continue to weave

Circulation of Consciousness
Endless Space Odyssey

Summer - the season of life - is over
Autumn - the season of silence - passes
At last - of death - the winter
And in spring we hear
The breath of new life

Inside our bodies
Without stopping a moment
The cycle of life and death continues

Observing the body from the atomic level
You are a completely different person
From what you were five years ago

Unchanged only is consciousness
I am not anyone else
I am my Identity

The consciousness that resides in our physical body
Eventually becomes particles of vapor
Carried by the wind
Exposed to the rain
Pouring down to the earth
Flowing the underground water veins
Life transcribed in flowing water
After a long period of time it returns to the sea
Consciousness drops from the vast ocean of the universe
Continuing the endless cosmic journey as it slowly rises

You are consciousness itself
I am consciousness itself

The Lifespan of Hope
Dedicated Seeker

I can empathize with a person's joy and happiness
When I see the pure heart in a person
That is where inspiration is born

Suspicion and jealousy
Will not bring inspiration

Seeking for where he should be
A dedicated seeker
Inspires people
Groping his way through a pitch-black world
The ray of hope
Will light up their footsteps

But the life of that light
Is not so long
To keep the flame of hope burning
You must be vigilant to move no matter
And above all, You must have courage

Take Courage
Run-up to cross the wall

How can we create "space?"
The answer is quite simple
Move as much as you can without space
Keep your mind and body active while you move

One day that will become flesh and blood and wisdom
It will bring you success
When you have accomplished, you will have confidence
You will have the strength to overcome
And that's when you will have a sense of freedom
That is where "space" is born

If you still can't overcome
Don't blame others or your environment
Have the courage to step back
And start running again
To overcome a wall
You need to run

Shoes and Pebbles
Dump the pebbles

Like a pebble in a shoe
To others it's insignificant
Small to others
To me, it's not so small
It happens all the time
But because of one such pebble
To let the splendor of a day fade
Would be quite foolish

No matter how hurried you are
Stop for a moment
Even if it takes a little longer
Take off your shoe and shake it upside down
Quickly throw away the pebble
That way you'll get to your destination
All the sooner
You'll get to your destination
And in comfort

Imaginary Journey
A magic carpet called imagination

Being alive means
To move
To move is to live
Because we are alive our hearts move
Because the heart moves, feelings are born
Those feelings move people
Motions make emotions
Create a new movement
Of people

The journey begins when people move
The purpose of the journey
To go somewhere other than here
To change one's environment
To change oneself
But a person
Can travel without moving
On a magic carpet
Called Imagination
One can fly anywhere in freedom

Afterword

When I was a child, going to play in the pine grove near my house was my greatest pleasure.

I was too small to reach the branches, but the older boys would pull me up. I could feel the rough, scaly bark of the tree. Inhaling the fresh green scent of the pine trees, I imagined myself flying in the sky on the back of a dragon god.

Whenever I went to the beach in front of the pine forest, I would always look for shells.

The hat that my mother had strictly ordered me to always wear to protect my head from the direct sunlight ended up becoming a container for rare shells and pine needles.

For me, the pine forests and beaches were a treasure house and sanctuary for new discoveries.

It was my father who instilled in me a curiosity and strong sense of adventure.

In contrast to my mother, who was a strict disciplinarian, my father, a playful and well-traveled man, gave me astronomy books, taught me where the constellations were, and showed me the vastness of the world before I even began elementary school. Even now, I could spend all day gazing at the sky and never get tired of it.

This book is a compilation of the thoughts I have written down from my childhood to the present while walking, swimming, resting, and sometimes lying down in the nature that surrounded me.

I have a brother who is five years younger than me. Unlike me, he is a quiet person. As an older sister, I envy him a lot, because I am quite overbearing. There is nothing good about being overbearing, but I always become so.

But he and I are very close, thanks to our parents. Instead of bequeathing any kind of property to us, they provided us with lots of education and experience. In this way I can be free from what is called "sibling rivalry."

That is what I intend to do with my children. I will only give them the strength to be independent and let them live their lives as they please.

I can say this now that it has been a long time since my father passed away.

There was a lot of conflict between me and my father before he died, but as soon as he was gone, I missed him. I feel more affection for him than anyone else, even though I disliked him so much in some ways. Now I think I understand a little why my mother loved my father so much, though.

My father lives inside me, my mother lives inside me, and my ancestors live inside me. I don't believe in a life of promises!

I want to shout aloud to the sky, "I live for adventure!"

Oh yes, this is something I am aware of every day.

They say that everything that happens in life is inevitable, but I disagree. I believe that this world is made up of a combination of "coincidences" and "inevitabilities," and it is a question of how to give meaning to "coincidences" that happen by chance. It is impossible to say to someone falling into the depths of despair is inevitable simply because of misfortune. The thought that everything is predetermined by fate is uninteresting! Human beings have the freedom to change "coincidence" into "inevitability." We can change our destiny as much as we want through free will. In life, if "coincidence" and "inevitability" always exist side by side, when a phenomenon appears, how do we interpret it ? That is what is important.

That is why I do not want to surrender myself to a predetermined fate.

I want to keep moving and working until I die. Simply because being able to do so is a very happy thing.

There is no lowly occupation, but there is a lowly way of life.

A lowly way of life rots the soul.

That's what my mother always told me. So, without fear of being misunderstood, I have the most faith in myself. I am quite egotistical, but I would not be able to do what I do if I did not know that. So in this book, I have written everything that I think from the bottom of my heart.

As the author, I would be more than happy if you could turn the pages and look through the book however you feel, no matter where you start.

Last but not least, I would like to thank the photographer Tateno Jiro for the wonderful photographs, Yamaoka Shigeru and Yamamoto Masakazu of Studio Give for their excellent bookbinding ideas, Iizuka Yukio, president of Iizuka Bookstore, who gave me the opportunity to publish the book, and Shirasaki Hiroshi, my advisor. Without any one of you, this book would not have been possible. I am sincerely grateful to all of them.

Kuniko FUJIYAMA

September 2022, on a lucky day

Profile

Kuniko FUJIYAMA

The special adviser to the Embassy of Republic of San Marino in Japan
Cavaliere of the Knights of St. Agata (the first Japanese woman)
Chairman of en art&design Inc.
Vice President of Kitayama Corporation
In 1989,She was Joined Virgin Atlantic,and employed locally as one of the "first Japanese international crew members", mainly responsible for upper class.
Certificate of Appreciation awarded by Mr. Nobuhisa Shimadzu, the Chief Priest of Terukuni Shrine on December 23, 2020.
Certificate of Appreciation awarded by Mr.Michihisa Kitashirakawa, the Chief Priest of Ise-shrine,Jinja Honcho on March 27,2015.
In April 2021 she travelled to Nara with the Ambassador Extraordinary and Plenipotentiary of the Republic of San Marino, Manlio Cadelo, who is also the head of the 157-nation diplomatic mission to Japan, and met with Mr. Fumon Sagawa, President of the Kegon sect and the 222nd and 223rd Betsuji priest of Todaiji.
She has had many contacts with important people and abroad in a wide range of fields including sports, the arts and politics. She is currently engaged in private diplomacy and actively organises online and other conferences on the theme of "Glocal" under the title of"Make a Better World".

The Grove of the Observer

November 1, 2022
First edition 1st printing published

Author	Kuniko FUJIYAMA
Photo	Jiro Tateno
Editor	Hiroshi Shirasaski
Design	Studio Give
Issuer	Yukio Iizuka
Publisher	Iizuka Shoten http://izbooks.co.jp
	5-16-4 koishikawa bunkyo-ku Tokyo
	112-0002 Japan
	Phone +81(0)3-3815-3805
	Mail iizuka@izbooks.co.jp
Printing	Shinano Publishing Press